Middle School Gratitude Journal for Girls

Girls gratitude journal to help middle school girls
think BIG, grow CONFIDENT, and love LIFE

This Book Belongs to:

_____

Middle School Gratitude Journal for Girls by Gratitude Daily
Published by Creative Ideas Publishing

For permissions contact:
permissions@creativeideaspublishing.com

ISBN: 978-1-952016-35-6

MiddLe ScHOOL WaS haRd FOR me

I moved school districts and had to make new friends. My feelings would sometimes sweep me off my feet. I had big curly hair that I didn't know how to style. I felt like an **OUTSideR** – like I wasn't as pretty as the other girls, didn't have the nicest clothes, or would never truly fit in. Somehow, I **SURViVed** middle school.

Many years later, I learned about a daily gratitude habit where each morning you spend time focusing on 3 things you are grateful for (whether big or small). I began to journal things I was grateful for, as well as, a goal I wanted to accomplish for the day. I kept at it each morning, and after just a week I began to feel **haPPieR** and more **CONFideNT**. Thinking about the good things in my life each day helps the negative thoughts become less and less.

I SO wish I had known about this habit as a middle schooler. That's why I want to share it with you. I don't want you to just survive middle school—I want you to thrive! And creating this daily gratitude habit now will help you **ThRiVe!**

ABOUT THE JOURNAL

1. You can journal about big things you are thankful for like family, friends, or an exciting adventure or you can be thankful for small things like a new book, sleeping late, or a new shirt.

2. Think of one important thing you can do for the day (finish homework before dinner, complete chores, not argue with a sibling, etc.), then think of how you can get that **ONE THING** done.

3. Take the time to think outside the box! Think big! Respond to the unique writing prompt each day.

4. I remember when I was in school, I would use the margins of my notebook paper to doodle, draw, make notes, write lists, or anything else that allowed my brain to express my thoughts, so I wanted to give you the same opportunity to let your brain express itself. You can use **"The Margin"** pages to be creative.

Here are a few important rules to help you thrive:

1. Commit to trying journaling for at least 14 days before deciding if it works or not.

2. If you miss a day, don't worry. Just journal tomorrow.

3. Breathe, relax, and have **FUN**!

Courage doesn't mean you don't get afraid. Courage means you don't let fear stop you.
-Bethany Hamilton *(Professional surfer)*

date: _____

I am thankful for:

1. _____ because _____
   _____

2. _____ because _____
   _____

3. _____ because _____
   _____

The ONE THING I need to do today is:

What is your favorite song? How do you feel after listening to it?

_____

_____

_____

_____

> To me, fearless is not the absence of fear. It's not being completely unafraid. To me, fearless is having fears. Fearless is having doubts. Lots of them. To me, fearless is living in spite of those things that scare you to death.
> -Taylor Swift

date: _____

I am thankful for:

1. _____ **because** _____

2. _____ **because** _____

3. _____ **because** _____

The ONE Thing I need to do today is:

Would it be better to be known by millions or to be highly respected by 100 people?

_____

_____

_____

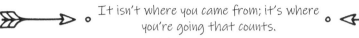

It isn't where you came from; it's where you're going that counts.

Ella Fitzgerald (First African-American woman to win a Grammy award)

date: _____

I am thankful for:

1. _____ because _____

_____

2. _____ because _____

_____

3. _____ because _____

_____

The ONE THING I need to do today is:

If you had the opportunity to be on the first ship to Mars, would you go? (Note: It takes 6 months to get to Mars.)

_____

_____

_____

Freeing yourself was one thing, claiming ownership of that freed self was another.
Toni Morrison (Author)

date: _____

I am thankful for:

1. _____ because _____

2. _____ because _____

3. _____ because _____

The ONE THING I need to do today is:

Who is one of your role models? Why?

_____

_____

_____

_____

I've learned that you can tell a lot about a person by the way (s)he handles these three things: rainy day, lost luggage, and tangled Christmas tree lights.
Maya Angelou (American poet and civil right activist)

date: _____

I am thankful for:

1. _____ because _____
_____

2. _____ because _____
_____

3. _____ because _____
_____

The ONE Thing I need to do today is:

Is there a trick or habit that would let you learn more in less time?

_____
_____
_____
_____

The Margin

We can push ourselves further. We
always have more to give.
Simone Biles (Olympic gymnast)

date: _____

I am thankful for:

1. _____ because _____

2. _____ because _____

3. _____ because _____

The ONE Thing I need to do today is:

What is something that you should do today that
you don't want to do?

_____

_____

_____

_____

The success of every woman should be the
inspiration to another. We should raise
each other up. Make sure you're very
courageous: be strong, be extremely kind,
and above all be humble.
Serena Williams

date: _____

I am thankful for:

1. _____ because _____

2. _____ because _____

3. _____ because _____

_____

The ONE Thing I need to do today is:

_____

Does anyone underestimate you? What do they
underestimate about you?

_____
_____
_____
_____

It's up to us to choose contentment and thankfulness now--and to stop imagining that we have to have everything perfect before we'll be happy.

Joanna Gaines   date: _____

I am thankful for:

1. _____ because _____

2. _____ because _____

3. _____ because _____

The ONE Thing I need to do today is:

Who is your favorite actor/actress? What is something they should improve?

_____

_____

_____

_____

I found I could say things with color and
shapes that I couldn't say any other
way--things I had no words for.
Georgia O'Keeffe *(Creator of a brand new
artistic movement)*

date: _____

I am thankful for:

1. _____ **because** _____

2. _____ **because** _____

3. _____ **because** _____

The ONE Thing I need to do today is:

[   ]

If you could give someone any gift, what would you give, who
would you give it to, and why would you give it to that person?

_____

_____

_____

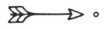

Change can happen when one least expects it. I know this to be true because my life changed in an instant.
Nadia Murad *(ISIS survivor and 2018 Nobel Peace Prize recipient)*

date: _____

I am thankful for:

1. _____ because _____

_____

2. _____ because _____

_____

3. _____ because _____

_____

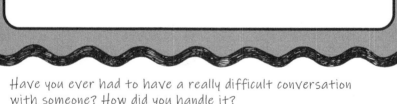

The **ONE Thing** I need to do today is:

Have you ever had to have a really difficult conversation with someone? How did you handle it?

_____

_____

_____

_____

The Margin

You don't learn anything from success,
but you learn a lot from your failures.
Gweynne Shotwell (COO of SpaceX)

date: _____

I am thankful for:

1. _____ because _____
_____

2. _____ because _____
_____

3. _____ because _____
_____

The ONE THING I need to do today is:

What is something that you do better than most people?

_____
_____
_____
_____

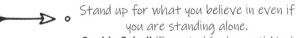 Stand up for what you believe in even if you are standing alone.
Sophie Scholl (*Executed for her anti-Nazi beliefs*)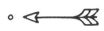

date: _____

I am thankful for:

1. _____ because _____
_____

2. _____ because _____
_____

3. _____ because _____
_____

The ONE Thing I need to do today is:

_____

Do you think your taste in music is set in stone or can it change in the future?

_____
_____
_____
_____

Don't let others define you. You define yourself.
Virginia Rometty (CEO of IBM)

date: _____

I am thankful for:

1. _____ because _____

2. _____ because _____

3. _____ because _____

The ONE Thing I need to do today is:

Where would you like to live in 10 years? Why?

_____

_____

_____

_____

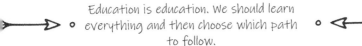

Education is education. We should learn everything and then choose which path to follow.
Malala Yousafzai (Education activist)

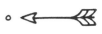

date: _____

I am thankful for:

1. _____ because _____

2. _____ because _____

3. _____ because _____

The ONE THING I need to do today is:

[ ]

If you only had 3 months to prepare for a high paying job, what career do you think you would be ready for?

_____

_____

_____

_____

Our words have power, but our actions
shape our lives.
Rachel Hollis (Author)

date: _____

I am thankful for:

1. _____ because _____
_____

2. _____ because _____
_____

3. _____ because _____
_____

The ONE Thing I need to do today is:

[   ]

If you had to live in another time period, what
time period would you choose?

_____
_____
_____
_____

date: _____

I am thankful for:

1. _____ because _____

2. _____ because _____

3. _____ because _____

The ONE Thing I need to do today is:

If you wanted a big allowance, what could you do to earn it?

_____

_____

_____

_____

Girls are capable of doing everything men are capable of doing. Sometimes they have more imagination than men.
Katherine Johnson
(mathematician and NASA scientist)

date: _____

I am thankful for:

1. _____ because _____

2. _____ because _____

3. _____ because _____

The ONE Thing I need to do today is:

_____

If you lived somewhere else in the solar system, where would it be?

_____

_____

_____

_____

Since I don't look like every other girl, it takes a while to be okay with that. To be different. But different is good.
Serena Williams

date: _____

I am thankful for:

1. _____ because _____
_____

2. _____ because _____
_____

3. _____ because _____
_____

The ONE Thing I need to do today is:

_____

What kind of traits do you want in a friend?

_____
_____
_____
_____

Failure is so important. We speak about success all the time. It is the ability to resist failure or use failure that often leads to greater success.
JK Rowling

date: _____

I am thankful for:

1. _____ because _____
_____

2. _____ because _____
_____

3. _____ because _____
_____

The ONE THING I need to do today is:

How do you reset your mind if you get angry, upset, or sad?

_____
_____
_____

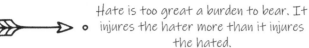

Hate is too great a burden to bear. It injures the hater more than it injures the hated.
Coretta Scott King (Wife of Martin Luther King Jr. and civil rights leader)

date: _____

I am thankful for:

1. _____ because _____

2. _____ because _____

3. _____ because _____

The ONE Thing I need to do today is:

Is there something that you could make and sell to start a business?

_____
_____
_____

Don't try so hard to fit in, and certainly don't try so hard to be different...just try hard to be you.
Zendaya

date: _____

I am thankful for:

1. _____ because _____
   _____

2. _____ because _____
   _____

3. _____ because _____
   _____

The ONE Thing I need to do today is:

```
[                                    ]
```

I am very proud because...

_____
_____
_____
_____

> A successful competition for me is always going out there and putting 100% into whatever I'm doing.
> **Simone Biles** (Olympic gymnast)

date: _____

I am thankful for:

1. _____ because _____

2. _____ because _____

3. _____ because _____

The ONE Thing I need to do today is:

_____

If you could live anywhere for 6 months, where would you go?

_____
_____
_____
_____

Everyone wants to win. But to truly succeed-
-whether it is at a sport or at your job or in
life--you have to be willing to do the hard work,
overcome the challenges, and make the sacrifices
it takes to be the best at what you do.
Rhonda Rousey (Professional fighter)

date: _____

I am thankful for:

1. _____ because _____

_____

2. _____ because _____

_____

3. _____ because _____

_____

The ONE Thing I need to do today is:

If you were given $150,000, what would you do
with the money?

_____

_____

_____

_____

> It takes humility to realize we don't know everything, not to rest on our laurels, and to know that we must keep learning and observing.
> **Cher Wang** (Co-Founder of HTC)

date: _____

I am thankful for:

♡ 1. _____ because _____

♡ 2. _____ because _____

♡ 3. _____ because _____

The ONE THING I need to do today is:

[   ]

What kind of job do you think you'd like to have in 20 years?

_____

_____

_____

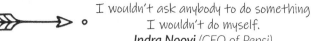

I wouldn't ask anybody to do something
I wouldn't do myself.
Indra Nooyi (CEO of Pepsi)

date: _____

I am thankful for:

1. _____ because _____

2. _____ because _____

3. _____ because _____

The ONE Thing I need to do today is:

[ ]

Why are computers and phones distracting?

_____
_____
_____

The Margin

date: _____

I am thankful for:

1. _____ **because** _____

2. _____ **because** _____

3. _____ **because** _____

The ONE Thing I need to do today is:

What are your favorite type of assignments or projects at school?

_____

_____

_____

_____

The future belongs to those who believe
in the beauty of their dreams.
Eleanor Roosevelt *(Former First Lady of
the United States)*

date: _____

I am thankful for:

1. _____ because _____

2. _____ because _____

3. _____ because _____

The ONE THING I need to do today is:

What would you try if you couldn't fail?

_____
_____
_____
_____

Leadership is not about popularity, it is about doing what is right.
Laura Bush (Former First Lady of the United States)

date: _____

I am thankful for:

1. _____ because _____

_____

2. _____ because _____

_____

3. _____ because _____

_____

The ONE Thing I need to do Today is:

_____

Who has helped you the most? How did they help you?

_____

_____

_____

_____

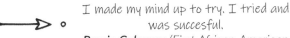 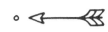

I made my mind up to try. I tried and was succesful.
Bessie Coleman *(First African-American woman to earn a pilot's license)*

date: _____

I am thankful for:

1. _____ because _____

2. _____ because _____

3. _____ because _____

The ONE THING I need to do today is:

Where is your favorite palce to be? Why?

_____

_____

_____

_____

Goals are only wishes unless you have a plan.
Melinda Gates

date: _____

I am thankful for:

1. _____ because _____

2. _____ because _____

3. _____ because _____

The ONE Thing I need to do today is:

Write a note to your future self.

_____

_____

_____

The Margin

Your success will have everything to do
with how you perceive yourself, because
how you perceive yourself is how others
will perceive you too.
Lori Greiner (Shark Tank investor)

date: _____

I am thankful for:

1. _____ because _____
_____

2. _____ because _____
_____

3. _____ because _____
_____

The ONE Thing I need to do today is:

What is your favorite form of exercise?

_____
_____
_____
_____

Life is full of what-ifs. You can't let it hold you back. If you do, you're not really living at all...just kind of going through the motions with no meaning.
Bethany Hamilton (Professional surfer)

date: _____

I am thankful for:

1. _____ because _____
_____

2. _____ because _____
_____

3. _____ because _____
_____

The ONE THING I need to do today is:

_____

How could you be a better student?

_____
_____
_____

Don't let anyone rob you of your imagination, your creativity, or your curiosity. It's your place in the world; it's your life. Go on and do all you can with it, and make it the life you want to live.
Mae Jemison *(First African-American woman to travel in space)*

date: _____

I am thankful for:

1. _____ because _____
_____

2. _____ because _____
_____

3. _____ because _____
_____

The ONE Thing I need to do today is:

What are you doing when you are the happiest?

_____
_____
_____
_____

True champions aren't always the ones that win, but those with the most guts
Mia Hamm *(Retired professional soccer player)*

date: _____

I am thankful for:

1. _____ because _____

2. _____ because _____

3. _____ because _____

The ONE THING I need to do today is:

If you had to go a day without a phone or social media what would you do?

_____

_____

_____

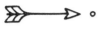 *Stand for something or you will fall for anything.*
Rosa Parks

date: _____

I am thankful for:

1. _____ because _____
_____

2. _____ because _____
_____

3. _____ because _____
_____

The ONE Thing I need to do today is:

what are the top 3 most important things in your life? What makes them special?

_____
_____
_____
_____

The Margin

In spite of everything. I still believe that people are really good at heart.
Anne Frank

date: _____

I am thankful for:

1. _____ because _____
_____

2. _____ because _____
_____

3. _____ because _____
_____

The ONE Thing I need to do today is:

If TV shows didn't exist, what would you do with your extra free time?

_____
_____
_____
_____

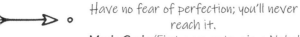 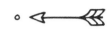

Have no fear of perfection; you'll never reach it.
Marie Curie *(First woman to win a Nobel Prize in physics and chemistry)*

date: _____

I am thankful for:

1. _____ because _____

2. _____ because _____

3. _____ because _____

The ONE THING I need to do today is:

what is your favorite thing about school? why?

_____
_____
_____
_____

I just knew if it could be done, it had to be done, and I did it.
Gertrude Ederle *(First woman to swim the English Channel)*

date: _____

I am thankful for:

1. _____ because _____

2. _____ because _____

3. _____ because _____

The ONE Thing I need to do today is:

Is there a subject you wish you were better at? What could you do to get better at it?

_____
_____
_____
_____

If you can't find happiness in the ugliness, you're not going to find it in the beauty, either.
Joanna Gaines

date: _____

I am thankful for:

1. _____ **because** _____
   _____

2. _____ **because** _____
   _____

3. _____ **because** _____
   _____

The ONE THING I need to do today is:

What is a habit you could start this week to make your life better in 6 months?

_____
_____
_____
_____

(He) said don't let them take you over. Walk into the room knowing you are the best. Shoulders back, chin up. Their attitudes will totally change.
Misty Copeland (American ballet dancer)

date: _____

I am thankful for:

1. _____ because _____

2. _____ because _____

3. _____ because _____

_____

The **ONE THING** I need to do today is:

What do you want people to say about you when you aren't around?

_____
_____
_____
_____

The Margin

Surround yourself only with people who are going to take you higher.
Oprah Winfrey

date: _____

I am thankful for:

1. _____ because _____
_____

2. _____ because _____
_____

3. _____ because _____
_____

The ONE Thing I need to do today is:

Do you prefer to read non-fiction or fiction books?

_____
_____
_____
_____

Hard days are the best because that's when champions are made. If you push through the hard days, then you can get through anything.
Gabby Douglas (Olympic gymnast)

date: _____

I am thankful for:

1. _____ because _____
_____

2. _____ because _____
_____

3. _____ because _____
_____

The ONE THING I need to do today is:

How could being bored be healthy for your brain?

_____
_____
_____
_____

Great minds discuss ideas; average minds discuss events; small minds discuss people.
Eleanor Roosevelt *(Former First Lady of the United States)*

date: _____

I am thankful for:

1. _____ because _____
_____

2. _____ because _____
_____

3. _____ because _____
_____

The ONE THING I need to do today is:

who is your favorite teacher? what makes him/ her your favorite?

_____
_____
_____
_____

> Be thankful for what you have; you'll end up having more. If you concentrate on what you don't have, you will never, ever have enough.
> **Oprah Winfrey**

date: _____

I am thankful for:

1. _____ because _____

_____

2. _____ because _____

_____

3. _____ because _____

_____

The ONE Thing I need to do Today is:

How would the world be different without social media?

_____

_____

_____

_____

Girls should never be afraid to be smart.
Emma Watson

date: _____

I am thankful for:

1. _____ because _____

2. _____ because _____

3. _____ because _____

The ONE Thing I need to do today is:

If you were given an extra hour in the day, what would you do with it?

_____
_____
_____
_____

The Margin

Happiness and confidence are the
prettiest things you can wear.
Taylor Swift

date: _____

I am thankful for:

1. _____ because _____

2. _____ because _____

3. _____ because _____

The ONE Thing I need to do today is:

What is your favorite book? Why?

_____

_____

_____

Follow your dreams. If you have a goal, and you want to achieve it, then work hard and do everything you can to get there, and one day it will come true.
Lindsey Vonn (World Cup ski racer)

date: _____

I am thankful for:

1. _____ because _____

2. _____ because _____

3. _____ because _____

The ONE THING I need to do today is:

List 5 personality traits you love about yourself.

_____

_____

_____

_____

Every great dream begins with a dreamer.
Harriet Tubman

date: _____

I am thankful for:

1. _____ because _____

2. _____ because _____

3. _____ because _____

The ONE Thing I need to do today is:

What is a goal or aspiration that no knows you have?

_____
_____
_____
_____

If everything was perfect, you would never learn and you would never grow.
Beyonce

date: _____

I am thankful for:

1. _____ because _____
_____

2. _____ because _____
_____

3. _____ because _____
_____

The ONE THING I need to do today is:

[   ]

What's something you do to make sure you are taking care of your health?

_____
_____
_____
_____

> Real integrity is doing the right thing,
> knowing that nobody's going to know
> whether you did it or not.
> *Oprah Winfrey*

date: _____

I am thankful for:

1. _____ because _____

2. _____ because _____

3. _____ because _____

The ONE Thing I need to do today is:

What does it mean to be successful in life?

_____

_____

_____

The Margin

It's so much better to promote what you love than to bash what you hate.
Jessica Alba

date: _____

I am thankful for:

1. _____ because _____
_____

2. _____ because _____
_____

3. _____ because _____
_____

The ONE Thing I need to do today is:

_____

What is a good reason to go to college?

_____
_____
_____
_____

Leadership is hard to define and good leadership even harder. But if you can get people to follow you to the ends of the earth, you are a great leader.
Indra Nooyi (CEO of Pepsi)

date: _____

I am thankful for:

1. _____ because _____

_____

2. _____ because _____

_____

3. _____ because _____

_____

The ONE THING I need to do today is:

_____

Why are computers and phones useful?

_____

_____

_____

_____

I know that in life there will be sickness, devastation, disappointments, heartache--it's a given. What's not given is the way you choose to get through it all. If you look hard enough, you can always find the bright side.
Rashida Jones

date: _____

I am thankful for:

1. _____ because _____

2. _____ because _____

3. _____ because _____

The ONE THING I need to do today is:

If you had $5,000, would your life be different? Why?

_____

_____

_____

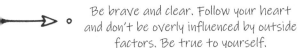 

Be brave and clear. Follow your heart and don't be overly influenced by outside factors. Be true to yourself.
Shirley Temple (Actress)

date: _____

I am thankful for:

1. _____ because _____

2. _____ because _____

3. _____ because _____

The ONE THING I need to do today is:

What is a meaningful gift you received? What made it special?

_____
_____
_____
_____

There is only one you. And there will never be another one. That's your power.
Mel Robbins (Author & speaker)

date: _____

I am thankful for:

1. _____ because _____
_____

2. _____ because _____
_____

3. _____ because _____
_____

The ONE Thing I need to do today is:

[ ]

What is something you could teach your peers about?

_____
_____
_____
_____

The Margin

You might not be able to control your circumstances, but you can control your response to your circumstances.
Condeleezza Rice (66th United States Secretary of State)

date: _____

I am thankful for:

1. _____ because _____
_____

2. _____ because _____
_____

3. _____ because _____
_____

The ONE Thing I need to do today is:

Brains grow by making mistakes. What's a mistake you made recently that you learned from?

_____
_____
_____
_____

To succeed in life, you need three things:
a wishbone, a backbone, and a funny
bone.
Reba McEntire (American singer)

date: _____

I am thankful for:

1. _____ because _____

2. _____ because _____

3. _____ because _____

The ONE Thing I need to do today is:

What is something you would do if you had unlimited money?
How much money does the thing you selected cost?

_____

_____

_____

_____

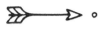 There's power in looking silly and not caring that you do.
Amy Pohler

date: _____

I am thankful for:

1. _____ because _____

2. _____ because _____

3. _____ because _____

The ONE Thing I need to do today is:

Who do you admire? Why?

_____
_____
_____
_____

You can catch a great attitude from great people.
Barbara Corcoran *(Shark Tank investor)*

date: _____

I am thankful for:

1. _____ because _____

2. _____ because _____

3. _____ because _____

The ONE THING I need to do today is:

What is the best advice you ever received?

_____

_____

_____

date: _____

I am thankful for:

1. _____ because _____
_____

2. _____ because _____
_____

3. _____ because _____
_____

The ONE THING I need to do today is:

What is something not taught in school that you think should be?

_____
_____
_____
_____

The Margin

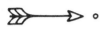

You, and only you, are ultimately
responsible for who you become and
how happy you are.
Rachel Hollis (Author)

date: _____

I am thankful for:

1. _____ because _____
_____

2. _____ because _____
_____

3. _____ because _____
_____

The ONE Thing I need to do today is:

What is something that you would like to read a
book about?

_____
_____
_____
_____

> It took me quite a long time to develop a voice, and now that I have it, I am not going to be silent.
> **Madeleine Albright** (First female United States Secretary of State)

date: _____

I am thankful for:

1. _____ because _____
   _____

2. _____ because _____
   _____

3. _____ because _____
   _____

The ONE THING I need to do today is:

_____

How would your life be different if you decided to stay off social media?

_____
_____
_____

Take a moment each day to focus on the good, and then try to carry that with you throughout the day, because while bangs don't look good on everyone, confidence does.

Lauren Conrad (Fashion designer)

date: _____

I am thankful for:

1. _____ because _____

2. _____ because _____

3. _____ because _____

_____

The ONE Thing I need to do today is:

What do other people like about you? Why does it make you unique?

_____

_____

_____

_____

I am my own muse. I am the subject I know best. The subject I want to better.
Frida Kahlo (Mexican painter)

date: _____

I am thankful for:

1. _____ because _____

2. _____ because _____

3. _____ because _____

The ONE Thing I need to do today is:

When do you prefer to talk on the phone instead of text?

_____

_____

_____

_____

If it doesn't scare you, you're
probably not dreaming big enough.
Tory Burch (Fashion designer)

date: _____

I am thankful for:

1. _____ because _____

2. _____ because _____

3. _____ because _____

The ONE Thing I need to do today is:

[   ]

What would you do to entertain your family
without spending any money?

_____

_____

_____

_____

The Margin

When you fall, get right back up. Just keep going, keep pushing it.
Lindsey Vonn (World Cup ski racer)

date: _____

I am thankful for:

1. _____ because _____

2. _____ because _____

3. _____ because _____

The ONE Thing I need to do today is:

What is an act of kindness someone showed you recently?

_____

_____

_____

_____

Take those chances and you can achieve greatness, whereas if you go conservative, you'll never know. I truly believe what doesn't kill you makes you stronger. Even if you fail, learning and moving on is sometimes the best thing.
Danica Patrick (American race driver)

date: _____

I am thankful for:

1. _____ because _____

_____

2. _____ because _____

_____

3. _____ because _____

_____

The ONE Thing I need to do today is:

List 10 places in the world that you would like to visit.

_____

_____

_____

_____

The power you have is to be the best
version of yourself you can be, so you can
create a better world.
Ashley Rickards (Actress)

date: _____

I am thankful for:

1. _____ because _____
_____

2. _____ because _____
_____

3. _____ because _____
_____

The ONE Thing I need to do today is:

If you were given $10,000 that you couldn't spend
on yourself, what would you spend it on?

_____
_____
_____
_____

Plan your work for today and every day,
then work your plan.
Margaret Thatcher (Britain's first female
prime minister)

date: _____

I am thankful for:

1. _____ because _____

2. _____ because _____

3. _____ because _____

The ONE THING I need to do today is:

who is someone that you should introduce yourself
to this week?

_____
_____
_____

You can't rely on how you look to sustain you, what sustains us, what is fundamentally beautiful is compassion; for yourself and for those around you.
Lupita Nyong'o

date: _____

I am thankful for:

1. _____ because _____

2. _____ because _____

3. _____ because _____

The ONE Thing I need to do today is:

How could you be a better friend?

_____

_____

_____

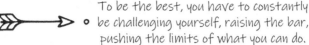

To be the best, you have to constantly be challenging yourself, raising the bar, pushing the limits of what you can do. Don't stand still, leap forward.
Rhonda Rousey *(Professional fighter)*

date: _____

I am thankful for:

1. _____ because _____
_____

2. _____ because _____
_____

3. _____ because _____
_____

The ONE Thing I need to do today is:

Are there any career options you might like if you couldn't go to college?

_____
_____
_____
_____

Make statements, with your actions
and your voice.
Tina Fey

date: _____

I am thankful for:

1. _____ because _____
_____

2. _____ because _____
_____

3. _____ because _____
_____

The ONE THING I need to do today is:

When having a discussion, is there any benefit to
listening to the person you disagree with? Why?

_____
_____
_____
_____

 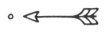

The best thing is to realize that you are who you are and you gotta work with what you got.
Zendaya

date: _____

I am thankful for:

1. _____ because _____

2. _____ because _____

3. _____ because _____

The ONE Thing I need to do today is:

If you could interview a movie star, who would you choose and why?

_____
_____
_____

For me, it is always important that I go through all the possible options for a decision.
Angela Merkel (Chancellor of Germany)

date: _____

I am thankful for:

1. _____ because _____

2. _____ because _____

3. _____ because _____

The ONE THING I need to do today is:

Who is someone that you could help today?

_____

_____

_____

_____

 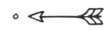

Nothing is impossible, the word itself
says 'I'm possible'!
Audrey Hepburn (Actress)

date: _____

I am thankful for:

1. _____ because _____

2. _____ because _____

3. _____ because _____

The ONE Thing I need to do today is:

If you could plan the best birthday party, what
would you do or have at the party?

_____

_____

_____

_____

The Margin

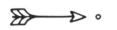

I went from thinking I could be a manager to thinking I could do something much bigger than that. **Geisha Williams** *(CEO of PG&E, first latina to run a Fortune 500 Company)*

date: _____

I am thankful for:

1. _____ because _____

2. _____ because _____

3. _____ because _____

The **ONE THING** I need to do today is:

What is your favorite birthday memory? What made it great?

_____
_____
_____
_____

Always be a first-rate version of
yourself, instead of a second-rate
version of somebody else.
Judy Garland (Starred in The Wizard
of Oz)

date: _____

I am thankful for:

1. _____ because _____
_____

2. _____ because _____
_____

3. _____ because _____
_____

The ONE Thing I need to do today is:

Is there a skill or task that others would be
willing to pay you to do?

_____
_____
_____
_____

Education is what allows you to stand out.
Ellen Ochoa *(First Hispanic woman in space)*

date: _____

I am thankful for:

1. _____ because _____

2. _____ because _____

3. _____ because _____

The ONE Thing I need to do today is:

What makes you a good friend?

_____

_____

_____

_____

I believe, every day, you should have
at least one exquisite moment.
Audrey Hepburn (Actress)

date: _____

I am thankful for:

1. _____ because _____

2. _____ because _____

3. _____ because _____

The ONE THING I need to do today is:

How have you changed since last school year?

_____
_____
_____

Traveling gives you some perspective
of what the rest of the world is like.
Meghan Markle

date: _____

I am thankful for:

1. _____ because _____

2. _____ because _____

3. _____ because _____

The ONE Thing I need to do today is:

If you had $5,000 to decorate your room, how
would you decorate it?

_____

_____

_____

_____

When something I can't control happens, I ask myself: where is the hidden gift, where is the positive in this?
Sara Blakely (Founder of Spanx)

date: _____

I am thankful for:

1. _____ because _____

2. _____ because _____

3. _____ because _____

The ONE Thing I need to do today is:

What historical figure would you like to hang out with?

_____

_____

_____

_____

Decide what you want. Declare it to the world. See yourself winning. And remember that if you are persistent as well as patient, you can get whatever you seek.

Misty Copeland (American ballet dancer)

date: _____

I am thankful for:

1. _____ because _____

_____

2. _____ because _____

_____

3. _____ because _____

_____

The ONE THING I need to do today is:

what is the benefit of having art in society?

_____

_____

_____

Being confident means believing in yourself. Ego means needing to prove that you're better than other people.
Barbara De Angelis

date: _____

I am thankful for:

1. _____ **because** _____

2. _____ **because** _____

3. _____ **because** _____

The ONE Thing I need to do today is:

what is an act of kindness you have shown someone?

_____

_____

_____

Your self-worth is determined by you.
You don't have to depend on someone
telling you who you are.
Beyonce

date: _____

I am thankful for:

1. _____ because _____
_____

2. _____ because _____
_____

3. _____ because _____
_____

The ONE THING I need to do today is:

When do you prefer to write by hand instead of
type on the computer?

_____
_____
_____

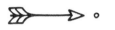

We can do no great things, only small things with great love.
Mother Teresa

date: _____

I am thankful for:

1. _____ because _____
   _____

2. _____ because _____
   _____

3. _____ because _____
   _____

The ONE THING I need to do today is:

What is a new responsibility that you are ready for?

_____
_____
_____
_____

The Margin

*You are wise when you listen,
especially to people with experience.*
Lori Greiner *(Shark Tank investor)*

date: _____

I am thankful for:

1. _____ because _____

2. _____ because _____

3. _____ because _____

The ONE Thing I need to do today is:

If you wrote a book, what would it be about?

_____

_____

_____

There are two ways of spreading
light. To be the candle, or the mirror
that reflects it.
Edith Wharton (Author)

date: _____

I am thankful for:

1. _____ because _____
_____

2. _____ because _____
_____

3. _____ because _____
_____

The ONE THING I need to do today is:

_____

If you had a spirit animal, what would it be?

_____
_____
_____
_____

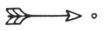

Feet, what do I need you for when I
have wings to fly?
Frida Kahlo (Mexican painter)

date: _____

I am thankful for:

1. _____ because _____

2. _____ because _____

3. _____ because _____

The ONE Thing I need to do today is:

If you wrote a quote or phrase to help motivate
yourself, what would it be?

_____

_____

_____

_____

Alone we can do so little; together we can do so much.
Helen Keller

date: _____

I am thankful for:

1. _____ because _____

2. _____ because _____

3. _____ because _____

The ONE THING I need to do today is:

If you had to cook dinner for your family tonight, what would you cook?

_____

_____

_____

_____

Work hard, push yourself, stay motivated and surround yourself with people that believe in you and your dreams.
Aly Raisman *(2-time Olympic gymnast)*

date: _____

I am thankful for:

1. _____ because _____

2. _____ because _____

3. _____ because _____

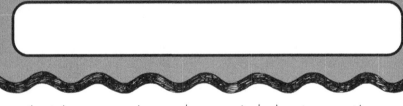

The ONE Thing I need to do today is:

What have you changed your mind about recently after receiving more information?

_____

_____

_____

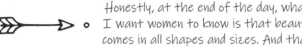

Honestly, at the end of the day, what I want women to know is that beauty comes in all shapes and sizes. And that it should not define who you are.
Ashley Graham (Model)

date: _____

I am thankful for:

1. _____ because _____

_____

2. _____ because _____

_____

3. _____ because _____

_____

The ONE Thing I need to do today is:

_____

what are 3 jobs you think will exist in 30 years, that don't exist now?

_____

_____

_____

_____

Everyone of us needs to show how
much we care for each other and, in
the process, care for ourselves.
Princess Diana

date: _____

I am thankful for:

1. _____ because _____
_____

2. _____ because _____
_____

3. _____ because _____
_____

The ONE THING I need to do today is:

What is something that you would like to learn
outside of school?

_____
_____
_____
_____

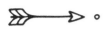

Life is not easy for any of us. But what of that? We must have perseverance and above all confidence in ourselves.
Marie Curie (First woman to win a Nobel Prize in physics and chemistry)

date: _____

I am thankful for:

1. _____ because _____

_____

2. _____ because _____

_____

3. _____ because _____

_____

The ONE Thing I need to do today is:

Beach vacation or ski trip? Why?

_____

_____

_____

_____

Be strong. Don't be a follower. Always
do the right thing.
Jennifer Lawrence

date: _____

I am thankful for:

1. _____ because _____

2. _____ because _____

3. _____ because _____

The ONE Thing I need to do today is:

What's your dream vacation? Where would you go,
what would you do, who would you take?

_____
_____
_____

Give yourself permission to shoot for something that seems totally beyond your grasp. You may be surprised at your capabilities.
Danica Patrick (American race driver)

date: _____

I am thankful for:

1. _____ because _____

2. _____ because _____

3. _____ because _____

The ONE Thing I need to do Today is:

If you could create a painting of your mood right now, what colors would you use and why?

_____

_____

_____

_____

The Margin

The most difficult thing is the decision to act. The rest is merely tenacity.
Amelia Earhart (first female aviator to fly solo across the Atlantic Ocean)

date: _____

I am thankful for:

1. _____ because _____
_____

2. _____ because _____
_____

3. _____ because _____
_____

The ONE Thing I need to do today is:

Who are you with when you are the most happy?

_____
_____
_____
_____

The whole world opened to me when I
learned to read.
Mary McLeod Bethune (Civil rights
activist for education)

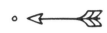

date: _____

I am thankful for:

1. _____ because _____
_____

2. _____ because _____
_____

3. _____ because _____
_____

The ONE Thing I need to do today is:

_____

If every job paid the same, what job would you
want to have?

_____
_____
_____
_____

I'm reading so much and exposing myself to so many new ideas. It almost feels like the chemistry and the structure of my brain is changing so rapidly sometimes.
Emma Watson

date: _____

I am thankful for:

1. _____ because _____

2. _____ because _____

3. _____ because _____

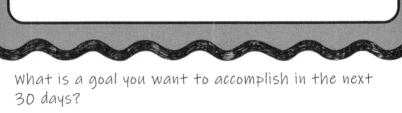

The ONE Thing I need to do Today is:

What is a goal you want to accomplish in the next 30 days?

_____

_____

_____

_____

The best way to show my gratitude
is to accept everything, even my
problems, with joy.
Mother Teresa

date: _____

I am thankful for:

1. _____ because _____
_____

2. _____ because _____
_____

3. _____ because _____
_____

The ONE THING I need to do today is:

What is something that you do well at school?

_____
_____
_____
_____

We've become conditioned to compromise and shrink ourselves in order to be liked. The problem is, when you work so hard to get everyone to like you, you very often end up not liking yourself so much.
Reshma Saujani (Creator of Girls Who Code)

date: _____

I am thankful for:

1. _____ because _____

2. _____ because _____

3. _____ because _____

The ONE Thing I need to do today is:

Is the pace of your day perfect? Too hectic or too slow?

_____

_____

_____

Thank YOU!

I hope you enjoyed your
100 days of gratitude journey!

Message or share your gratitude journey with us on
Instagram @CreativeIdeasPublishing

Share The Gift OF Gratitude With a Friend OR Family Member!

Made in the USA
Las Vegas, NV
22 November 2022